SPORTS
DYNASTIES

MIKE
KRZYZEWSKI

AND THE DUKE
BLUE DEVILS

abdopublishing.com

Published by Abdo Publishing, a division of ABDO, PO Box 398166, Minneapolis, Minnesota 55439.
Copyright © 2019 by Abdo Consulting Group, Inc. International copyrights reserved in all countries.
No part of this book may be reproduced in any form without written permission from the publisher.
SportsZone™ is a trademark and logo of Abdo Publishing.

Printed in the United States of America, North Mankato, Minnesota
042018
092018

THIS BOOK CONTAINS
RECYCLED MATERIALS

Distributed in paperback by North Star Editions, Inc.

Cover Photos: Rich Graessle/Icon Sportswire/AP Images, left; Mark J. Terrill/AP Images, right
Interior Photos: Rich Graessle/Icon Sportswire/AP Images, 4–5; Chris Steppig/NCAA Photos/AP Images,
6; Mark J. Terrill/AP Images, 8; Bettmann/Getty Images, 10–11; Heinz Kluetmeier/Sports Illustrated/Getty
Images, 12; Gerry Broome/AP Images, 14–15, 22; Bob Jordan/AP Images, 17; Charles Rex Arbogast/AP
Images, 19; Chris Gardner/AP Images, 21, 42; Chuck Burton/AP Images, 24; Eric Risbery/AP Images, 26–27;
Charles Arbogast/AP Images, 28; David Gonzales/NCAA Photos/Getty Images, 31; Pool/KRT/Newscom,
32; Mark Cornelison/MCT/Newscom, 35; Robin Alam/Icon Sportswire/AP Images, 36; Chris Williams/Icon
Sportswire/AP Images, 38–39; Mel Evans/AP Images, 41

Editor: Bradley Cole
Series Designer: Craig Hinton

Library of Congress Control Number: 2017962592

Publisher's Cataloging-in-Publication Data

Names: Glave, Tom, author.
Title: Mike Krzyzewski and the Duke Blue Devils / by Tom Glave.
Description: Minneapolis, Minnesota : Abdo Publishing, 2019. | Series: Sports dynasties | Includes online
    resources and index.
Identifiers: ISBN 9781532114359 (lib.bdg.) | ISBN 9781641852845 (pbk) | ISBN 9781532154188 (ebook)
Subjects: LCSH: Krzyzewski, Mike, 1947-.--Juvenile literature. | Basketball coaches--United States-
    -Biography--Juvenile literature. | Basketball--Juvenile literature. | Duke Blue Devils (Basketball
    team)--Juvenile literature.
Classification: DDC 796.323092 [B]--dc23

TABLE OF
CONTENTS

CHAPTER 1

NEEDING EVERY
LAST MINUTE

Time seemed to stand still as the basketball flew through the air. The final shot sailed toward the basket, and the buzzer sounded. The 71,000 fans were nearly silent as the ball hit the backboard. It bounced off the rim and fell to the floor. Butler's half-court shot had missed. Duke won 61–59. They were the best college team in the country.

Duke was back on top of the college basketball world. It was the school's fourth

Mike Krzyzewski coaches his team from the sideline during the 2010 national championship season.

Kyle Singler fights for a rebound against Butler.

national championship under coach Mike Krzyzewski. The
Blue Devils fought hard for a big win to cap a magical season.
The victory showed why the Duke Blue Devils were the best
college basketball team around. The Blue Devils have won
lots of games under Krzyzewski. The win against Butler on
April 5, 2010, came down to the final shot.

"They weren't going to go away," Duke junior forward
Kyle Singler said after the game. "We needed every last minute
of that game to get this win."

Butler entered the championship match on a 25-game winning streak. The game was played just six miles (9.7 km) from the Butler campus. It seemed that everyone wanted to see the Bulldogs win.

Duke had been knocked out of the National Collegiate Athletic Association (NCAA) tournament early the previous three seasons. This group of seniors wanted a chance to win the national championship. They earned a top seed and easily advanced to the final.

Butler was a tough team. It stayed close to Duke the whole game. The Blue Devils' biggest lead of the game was six points after Singler's jumper with five minutes left in the first half. Then Butler scored seven quick points to take the lead. Nolan Smith's three-pointer a few minutes later gave Duke a 33–32 halftime lead. The game remained close throughout the second half.

Duke senior Jon Scheyer was fouled on a layup with eight minutes left in the game. The layup went in, and he hit the free throw to give the Blue Devils a five-point lead.

The Duke lead was still five points with three minutes left. Butler's Matt Howard scored twice to cut the lead to 60–59. Then a rebound went off the foot of Duke center Brian Zoubek

Butler's Gordon Hayward heaves the last shot of the 2010 national championship game against Duke.

in the final minute to give the ball to the Bulldogs. Butler called timeout to set up a shot. The Bulldogs then used their final timeout when they could not inbound the ball.

Gordon Hayward, Butler's star forward, tried to drive in for a bucket. He spun away from Singler. He had to shoot his fadeaway high over the 7-foot-1-inch Zoubek. The shot missed, and Zoubek grabbed the rebound. He was quickly fouled with 3.6 seconds left.

HOME, SWEET INDY

Three of Duke's championships under coach Mike Krzyzewski have been won in Indianapolis. The first was at the Hoosier Dome. The 2010 and 2015 titles were won at Lucas Oil Stadium. Duke's other two titles were both won at the Metrodome in Minneapolis.

Zoubek made the first foul shot for a two-point lead. He was told by Krzyzewski to miss the second foul shot. Krzyzewski wanted to make sure Butler would not have enough time to set up a final play. Hayward leaped to grab the rebound and raced toward midcourt for the final shot.

The shot rattled out of the rim, and the Duke players jumped in excitement. The Duke coaching staff hugged Krzyzewski after his gutsy free-throw call.

CHAPTER 2

THE KRZYZEWSKI ERA BEGINS

D uke University was looking for a new basketball coach in 1980. Bill Foster had left to take a new job at the University of South Carolina. He had built a 113–64 record in six seasons at Duke. Foster led the Blue Devils to three NCAA tournaments. They played in the 1978 national championship game.

Duke's director of athletics, Tom Butters, was looking for someone to build on that success. He interviewed an unknown young coach who

Mike Krzyzewski answers questions after being hired as the head coach of Duke's men's basketball program.

Johnny Dawkins scores against top-seeded North Carolina in the 1984 ACC tournament.

didn't immediately impress him. Krzyzewski had just finished a 9–17 season at Army. Krzyzewski left and headed to the airport. Butters changed his mind and decided to hire Krzyzewski. It turned out to be the smartest decision he ever made.

At 33 years old, Krzyzewski was hired on March 18, 1980. He had a 38–47 record in his first three seasons. Some fans were disappointed with the results. But Butters stuck with Krzyzewski.

The Blue Devils set an NCAA record with 37 wins in the 1985–86 season. The loss to Louisville in the national championship ended a 21-game winning streak. Kentucky broke the record in 2012 when it won 38 games.

Krzyzewski's third season ended with a 109–66 loss to Virginia in the Atlantic Coast Conference (ACC) Tournament. He called it a pivotal moment in his career. At dinner someone started a toast about forgetting the loss. But Krzyzewski said they should never forget that game. When Duke returned to practice the next fall, the scoreboard read "109–66."

That team laid the foundation of Duke's future. Players like Johnny Dawkins and Jay Bilas returned for the 1983–84 season. They won 24 games the next season. They beat the No. 1 seed in the ACC tournament, the University of North Carolina (UNC). The Blue Devils went to the NCAA tournament for the first time under Krzyzewski. Blue Devils lost that year to Washington in their first NCAA tournament game.

Two years later, the 1985–86 Blue Devils made a run at the NCAA championship game, but lost to Louisville 72–69. This tough loss would be followed by great success.

CHAPTER 3

BUILDING A DYNASTY

Krzyzewski has won more games than any other basketball coach in NCAA history. He broke the record of Bobby Knight, the coach at the University of Indiana. Knight was also Krzyzewski's mentor and had hired him as an assistant at Army. A win against Michigan State gave him win No. 903 to pass Knight. Krzyzewski became the first men's basketball coach to win 1,000 career games in 2015.

Mike Krzyzewski is recognized for breaking the NCAA career wins record for men's basketball in 2011.

Krzyzewski's Duke teams missed the NCAA tournament just once between 1984 and 2017. His five national championships with the Blue Devils are second behind University of California, Los Angeles (UCLA) coach John Wooden's 10.

Much of Duke's success has been attributed to Krzyzewski's leadership and recruiting. He looks for players who are not only good athletes but also good leaders. He teaches his teams to play together. His style is shaped by his military background, but he's flexible enough to adjust to the players on his roster.

No coach can win without great players. And Krzyzewski's ability to recruit top athletes helped launch and maintain the Duke dynasty.

THE FOUNDATION

The second recruiting class included Johnny Dawkins. The 6-foot-2-inch guard led Duke in scoring all four years he played. He won the Naismith College Player of the Year award as a senior. That award is given to the best college basketball player in the county. A Duke player has won that award six more times.

The Henry Iba Corinthian Award was renamed the National Association of Basketball Coaches (NABC) Defensive Player of

Danny Ferry was one of Krzyzewski's first superstars at Duke.

the Year Award. Tommy Amaker won the award as a senior

in 1987. A Blue Devil has won it eight more times. Teammate

Billy King won it after Amaker.

FERRY'S FIRST

In 1989 Danny Ferry, a 6-foot-10-inch forward, was a big part of another group of successful seniors. Ferry was a great outside shooter and all-around player. He led Duke in scoring for three straight years. He was named the best player in the ACC. Ferry was also named National Player of the Year. Ferry was the first ACC player to record 2,000 points, 1,000 rebounds, and 500 assists in a career.

LAETTNER LEADS

A core group of players helped Duke win consecutive national titles in 1991 and 1992. Christian Laettner led the Blue Devils in scoring in both championship seasons. Laettner was named the Most Outstanding Player at the Final Four in 1991. He led Duke with 21.5 points and 7.9 rebounds as a senior in 1992. He was named the National Player of the Year. As a forward, he dominated inside but also hit almost half of his three-point shots over his four years at Duke.

Bobby Hurley was named the Most Outstanding Player at the Final Four in 1992. Hurley was an outstanding point guard and had excellent court vision. His passing helped teammates Christian Laettner and Grant Hill score.

Christian Laettner was an outstanding scorer and rebounder for the Blue Devils.

Hill was named an All-American in 1994. He played alongside Laettner for two years and Hurley for three years. He was the Blue Devils' top scorer in two seasons. He played point guard when Hurley was injured. Hill threw a long pass to Laettner in the 1992 game against Kentucky that set up Laettner's famous game-winning shot. He was named the Defensive Player of the Year in 1993.

BATTIER'S THE BEST

Shane Battier was named the country's best defensive player three years in a row. Only two other players have won that award three times. Battier helped the Blue Devils win the national championship in 2001. He was named the best player at the Final Four. He averaged 19.9 points that year. Battier also had 82 steals and 88 blocked shots. He was named the National Player of the Year and Defensive Player of the Year at the same time. Only three other players have ever done that.

SCORING DUO

Jason Williams led Duke in scoring during the 2001 national title season. He scored 17 straight points against UCLA in an NCAA tournament game. Williams and Battier were the first Duke duo to each score 700 points in the same season. Williams led Duke in scoring again in 2002. He was named the country's best player.

SCORING MACHINE

Williams was a great scorer, but his records didn't last long. J. J. Redick set scoring records from all over the floor. Redick led Duke in scoring in 2005 and 2006. He was named the ACC's

best player both years. He was known for his success at the free-throw line and the three-point line.

He was named the Naismith Player of the Year in 2006. Redick broke Jason Williams's school record for single season points and total points. Redick scored 964 in 2006. He finished with 2,769 points in his career. That was a record both for Duke and for the ACC. His free-throw shooting helped him set those marks. He also set the NCAA career record for three-point field goals. Redick left his name all over the Duke record books.

BIG BLOCKS

Shelden Williams might have been Duke's best defensive player since Battier. Williams won back-to-back NABC Defensive Player of the Year awards in 2005 and 2006. He averaged more than 10 rebounds both seasons. But Williams wasn't just a threat on the defensive end of the floor.

Jon Scheyer, Kyle Singler, and Nolan Smith were the nation's top-scoring trio in 2010. They led Duke to the national title that year. Scheyer and Singler became the second Duke duo to each score 700 points.

Jabari Parker shoots against Mercer during the second round of the NCAA tournament.

Mason Plumlee finished his career in 2013 with more than 1,000 points and 1,000 rebounds. He played with his brothers Miles and Marshall at Duke.

Only two Duke players have averaged a double-double for an entire season under Krzyzewski. Shelden Williams was the first, and he did it again as a senior. Mason Plumlee did it in 2013.

YOUNG LEADERS

Freshman Jabari Parker led Duke in scoring in 2013–2014. He was named the country's best freshman player in his only season at Duke.

Three freshmen joined senior Quinn Cook to lead Duke to the 2015 national title. Jahlil Okafor averaged a team-best 17.3 points. He was named National Freshman of the Year. Okafor was the first freshman to be named the ACC's best player.

Freshman Tyus Jones was named the Most Outstanding Player at the Final Four. Freshman Justise Winslow averaged 12.6 points and also had an outstanding NCAA tournament. Freshman Grayson Allen was a big contributor on the national title team and led the Blue Devils in scoring the next season.

CHAPTER 4

THE CHAMPIONSHIP SEASONS

The Blue Devils lost in the Final Four in 1988 and 1989. The next year, Duke ran into a powerful University of Nevada Las Vegas (UNLV) team. UNLV crushed Duke by 30 points in the championship. Duke fans began to wonder if they would ever get over the hump.

In 1990–91 sixth-ranked Duke and No. 4 North Carolina were tied for first place in the ACC with one game left. The Blue Devils traveled the 10 miles (16 km) from Durham to Chapel Hill

Larry Johnson was part of the great UNLV teams that battled with Duke in the early 1990s.

Christian Laettner launches the game-winning shot against Kentucky.

to play UNC. The Blue Devils beat the Tar Heels 83–77 to steal the regular-season title from their archrivals.

The Blue Devils were awarded a No. 2 seed in the NCAA tournament. Bobby Hurley scored 20 points in a win against

St. John's to send Duke to the Final Four. This time the Blue Devils were ready for the undefeated UNLV. Duke ruined UNLV's perfect season with a 79–77 victory.

Hurley came up big again in the title game against Kansas. He hit Grant Hill for an alley-oop dunk early in the game for one of his nine assists on the night. Duke built a double-digit lead in the second half. Laettner hit all 12 of his free throws and finished with 18 points. Duke beat Kansas 72–65 for its first national championship.

LAETTNER'S ENCORE

Duke was back again a year later after winning 25 games in the 1991–92 regular season. Laettner continued a strong senior season with 25 points, 10 rebounds, and seven steals as Duke beat North Carolina for the ACC tournament title.

The matchup with Kentucky in the Elite Eight would prove to be Duke's greatest test yet. Kentucky rallied to force an overtime period. Guard Sean Woods gave the Wildcats a 103–102 lead with 2.1 seconds left. The Blue Devils were going to need nothing short of a miracle.

Grant Hill inbounded the ball from underneath his own basket. His long pass found Laettner near the foul line. Laettner faked to his right and spun to his left. Then he shot a 15-foot fadeaway as time expired. The ball found the net. The Blue Devils went crazy as the 104–103 win sent them to the Final Four.

Duke used a big second-half run to down Indiana in the semifinal. Then the Blue Devils defense clamped down on Michigan in the title game. Laettner scored 19 points and Hill had 18 as Duke repeated as national champions with a 71–51 victory.

Laettner moved on after that game, and Hurley followed a year later. Hill led Duke back to the national title game in 1994, but top-ranked Arkansas came away with a four-point

ONE AND DONE

Now many of the nation's best players leave after their freshman year for the NBA Draft. This has made creating a lasting dynasty even harder today. Each year star players have to be replaced with new recruits rather than staying on for four years.

Guard Trajan Langdon shoots over Connecticut defender in the 1999 national championship game.

win. Krzyzewski missed most of the next season following back surgery.

BACK ON TOP

The team struggled in Krzyzewski's absence. But it proved to be just a minor setback. The Blue Devils won four straight

Shane Battier, known for his defense, dunks against Maryland during a Final Four game in 2001.

ACC regular-season titles from 1997 to 2000. They also won the conference tournament five straight seasons starting in 1999.

The 1998–99 team tied a program record with 37 wins and went undefeated in conference play. That Duke team also won a school-record 32 straight games. In the national title game against Connecticut, Duke guard Trajan Langdon scored 25 points. Center Elton Brand added 15 points and 13 rebounds. Langdon's three-pointer got Duke within 73–72 with 1:30 left. But a late turnover spoiled Duke's comeback attempt. The winning streak ended in the national championship game with a 77–74 loss to Connecticut.

A string of exciting wins led the Blue Devils to the tournament again in 2001. Nate James and Jason Williams combined for 13 points in the final minute to force overtime at Maryland in January. Shane Battier had six points and a blocked shot in the extra period to help Duke win.

Chris Duhon hit a buzzer-beater at Wake Forest. James had a tip-in to beat Maryland in the ACC tournament. Duke won the tournament by beating rival North Carolina in the final.

The Blue Devils faced Maryland again in the national semifinals. They trailed by 22 points in the first half but they stormed back. Williams's three-pointer put them ahead for good with seven minutes left.

Battier played all 40 minutes in the championship game against Arizona. He finished with 18 points and 11 rebounds. Mike Dunleavy drained five three-pointers to help Duke win. Carlos Boozer added 12 points and 12 rebounds. Duke won 82–72 for its third title.

Duke continued its success in the NCAA tournament. The Blue Devils went to the Sweet Sixteen six times in the next eight seasons between 2002 and 2009. The 2004 season included a trip to the Final Four.

UNSUNG HEROES

The 2009–10 roster didn't have a lot of big stars. But tough defense and rebounding helped lead an overlooked team to the national title. Duke allowed just 61 points per game that season.

Brian Zoubek moved into the starting lineup late in the season with just 17 games and 16 rebounds. His rebounding added to the great scoring of Jon Scheyer, Kyle Singler, and Nolan Smith. Duke shared the regular-season ACC title and won the conference tournament thanks to Scheyer's late three-pointer.

Freshman Tyus Jones shoots a layup against Wisconsin in the 2015 national championship.

Scheyer, Singler, and Smith combined for 63 points in a big win against West Virginia in the Final Four. That set up the exciting title game against Butler. The trio combined for 47 points in the two-point win over the Bulldogs.

Duke suffered some early exits from the NCAA tournament until it won the national title again in 2015. Duke beat No. 1 Wisconsin by 10 early in the season. The Blue Devils were their region's top seed in the NCAA tournament. They advanced to the Final Four with ease. Freshman Justise Winslow had 19 points in the semifinal win over Michigan State.

The title game was a rematch with Wisconsin. Duke trailed late in the game. Wisconsin had a nine-point lead with 13 minutes left. Freshman Grayson Allen started the comeback by scoring Duke's next eight points. Freshman Jahlil Okafor had two buckets, and Jones hit two three-pointers to put Duke ahead for good in the final minutes.

Freshman Tyus Jones finished the game with 23 points. Duke's four freshmen combined for 60 of the team's 68 points. With these freshmen, three more years of championships seemed like a sure thing. But now many of the nation's best players leave after their freshman year for the National Basketball Association (NBA). This has made creating a lasting dynasty even harder today.

CHAPTER 5

BASKETBALL AFTER DUKE

Krzyzewski's success at Duke gave him a special opportunity. He was named the head coach of the United States National Basketball Team in 2005. He led the team to an 88–1 record and three Olympic gold medals. Team USA won Olympic gold in 2008, 2012, and 2016.

Krzyzewski has also been recognized several times for his success. He was inducted into the Naismith Basketball Hall of Fame in 2001. He is

Mike Krzyzewski coaches Team USA in an exhibition game against China in 2016.

also in the Army Sports Hall of Fame and Duke Athletics Hall of Fame.

DUKE AT THE DRAFT

Through 2017 the Duke basketball team has had 57 players picked in the NBA Draft during the Krzyzewski era. That includes 35 players selected in the first round of the draft. Duke also has a record 23 players selected by lottery teams. Danny Ferry was Duke's first lottery pick in 1989. He was picked second by the Los Angeles Clippers.

In 1999 Elton Brand became the first Duke player picked No. 1 overall. Trajan Langdon, Corey Maggette, and William Avery were also selected in the first round in 1999. That was the first time four players from the same school were picked in the first round.

Jason Williams was the second overall pick of the 2002 NBA Draft. Duke teammate Mike Dunleavy was picked third. It was the second time in NBA history that two teammates were selected in the top three picks.

Kyrie Irving was the No. 1 pick by the Cleveland Cavaliers in 2011. Brand (2000), Irving (2012), and Grant Hill (1995) won NBA

Kyrie Irving is selected first in the 2011 NBA draft coming out of Duke.

Rookie of the Year awards. Irving and Dahntay Jones won an NBA championship with Cleveland in 2016. Shane Battier won NBA titles with the Miami Heat in 2012 and 2013, and Ferry won an NBA title with the San Antonio Spurs in 2003.

Johnny Dawkins, *left,* **Steve Wojciechowski,** *center,* **and Chris Collins,** *right,* are all part of the Coach K coaching tree.

Jahlil Okafor and Justise Winslow were lottery picks in 2015 after their freshman year at Duke. Brandon Ingram and Jayson Tatum followed them in 2016 and 2017.

Duke retires the jersey numbers of players that earn national recognition during their time at Duke and earn a degree. Nine of Krzyzewski's players have had their numbers retired: Johnny Dawkins, Danny Ferry, Christian Laettner, Bobby Hurley, Grant Hill, Shane Battier, Jason Williams, Shelden Williams, and J. J. Redick.

Several of Krzyzewski's players have also become basketball coaches. Five are head coaches of college teams. Steve Wojciechowski coaches at Marquette, and Chris Collins coaches at Northwestern. Tommy Amaker is the Harvard coach, and Johnny Dawkins coaches at Central Florida. Bobby Hurley coaches Arizona State. Former Duke assistant Mike Brey is the head coach at Notre Dame as well.

Quin Snyder became the head coach of the NBA's Utah Jazz in 2014. Grant Hill is one of the owners of the NBA's Atlanta Hawks. Trajan Langdon and Ferry work for other NBA teams.

Krzyzewski has also kept former players in the program at Duke. Jeff Capel, Nate James, Jon Scheyer, and Nolan Smith were on his 2017–18 coaching staff.

HOME COURT ADVANTAGE

During the 2000–2001 season, Duke named the basketball court at Cameron Indoor Stadium, Coach K Court. Duke has a 504–63 record at Cameron Indoor Stadium under Krzyzewski. The Blue Devils have sold out the Stadium for 422 straight games. Duke set a school record with 46 straight home wins between January 1997 and February 2000.

DUKE BLUE DEVILS

SPAN OF DYNASTY

- 1990–91 to present

KEY RIVALS

- North Carolina, Maryland, Michigan, Georgia Tech, Kansas

HEAD COACH

- Record under Krzyzewski: 1027–279
- ACC Record under Krzyzewski: 414–184

NCAA TOURNAMENT

- NCAA tournament appearances: 34
- Final Four appearances: 12
- Title game appearances: 10
- National championships: 1991, 1992, 2001, 2010, 2015 (seasons)

AWARDS FOR KRZYZEWSKI

- ACC Coach of the Year: 5
- National Coach of the Year: 9
- USA Basketball National Coach of the Year: 7
- Naismith Memorial Basketball Hall of Fame: Inducted in 2001

INDIVIDUAL AWARDS

NAISMITH COLLEGE PLAYER OF THE YEAR

- Johnny Dawkins (1986)
- Danny Ferry (1989)
- Christian Laettner (1992)
- Elton Brand (1999)
- Shane Battier (2001)
- Jason Williams (2002)
- J. J. Redick (2006)

WOODEN AWARD

- Christian Laettner (1992)
- Elton Brand (1999)
- Shane Battier (2001)
- Jason Williams (2002)
- J. J. Redick (2006)

ASSOCIATED PRESS PLAYER OF THE YEAR

- Christian Laettner (1992)
- Elton Brand (1999)
- Shane Battier (2001)
- Jason Williams (2002)
- J. J. Redick (2006)

RCH 18, 1980

Mike Krzyzewski is hired to coach the Duke men's basketball team.

RIL 1, 1991

Duke beats Kansas 72–65 for its first national championship.

RIL 6, 1992

Duke beats Michigan 71–51 for its second national championship.

NE 30, 1999

Duke is the first school in the history to have four players selected in the first round of the NBA Draft.

RIL 2, 2001

Duke beats Arizona 82–72 on April 2 for its third national championship.

TOBER 5, 2001

Krzyzewski is inducted into the Naismith Memorial Basketball Hall of Fame.

APRIL 5, 2010

Duke beats Butler 61–59 for its fourth national championship.

NOVEMBER 15, 2011

Krzyzewski passes former coach Bob Knight for most Division I basketball wins, winning his No. 903.

JANUARY 25, 2015

Krzyzewski becomes the first Division I basketball coach with 1,000 career victories.

APRIL 6, 2015

Duke beats Wisconsin 68–63 for its fifth national championship.

MARCH 25, 2018

Duke falls in Elite Eight to Kansas, one game short of returning to another Final Four appearance.

GLOSSARY

ALL-AMERICAN
Designation for players chosen as the best amateurs in the country in a particular sport.

BACKBOARD
The upright panel that holds the basketball basket.

CHAMPIONSHIP
A contest held to find the winner of a league.

COMEBACK
When a team losing a game rallies to tie the score or take the lead.

CONFERENCE
A group of schools that join together to create a league for their sports teams.

CONSECUTIVE
Following one after the other in a series.

DOUBLE-DOUBLE
Accumulating 10 or more of two certain statistics in a game.

DRAFT
A system that allows teams to acquire new players coming into a league.

FRESHMAN
A first-year player.

REBOUND
When a player gains control of the basketball after a missed shot.

RECRUIT
To catch the ball after a shot has been missed.

ROOKIE
A professional athlete in his or her first year of competition.

SENIOR
A student in his or her fourth year of college.

ONLINE RESOURCES

Booklinks
NONFICTION NETWORK
FREE! ONLINE NONFICTION RESOURCES

To learn more about Mike Krzyzewski and the Duke Blue Devils, visit abdobooklinks.com. These links are routinely monitored and updated to provide the most current information available.

BOOKS

Ervin, Phil. *Total Basketball*. Minneapolis, MN: Abdo Publishing, 2017.

Howell, Brian. *Duke Blue Devils*. Minneapolis, MN: Abdo Publishing, 2012.

Wilner, Barry. *The Greatest Coaches of All Time*. Minneapolis, MN: Abdo Publishing, 2016.

INDEX

ABOUT THE AUTHOR

Tom Glave studied journalism at the University of Missouri. He has written about sports for newspapers in New Jersey, Missouri, Arkansas, and Texas. He has also written several books about sports. He looks forward to teaching his children about all kinds of sports.